Can I talk to a chimpanzee?

Contents

Written by Peter Gallivan

Collins

1 What is communication?

So much of our time is spent communicating with each other – having a chat with a friend, waving hello to a neighbour, sending a text. Communication is really just sending and receiving messages. These messages help us to work together, share ideas and learn from each other. Our survival depends on it, all across the world.

But it isn't only humans that communicate. It's vital to animals too. A chimpanzee grunting, a dog sniffing and even a deer's impressive antlers are all ways of communicating. A grunt might keep a family safe, a sniff might make a friendship and impressive antlers might help find a partner. These are just some of the many different ways of communication to be found across the animal kingdom.

Deer use their large antlers to tell others how strong they are.

Picking up signals

Animals need to know what is happening around them in order to do anything, from finding food to spotting a dangerous **predator**. Just like humans, animals have special body parts which can detect what's going on in different ways. These are known as senses.

 sight: eyes detect light and see what's around

 hearing: ears collect sound in order to hear things

 smell: noses identify odours to smell things

 touch: skin senses the touch of something

 taste: tongues detect what things taste like

Senses aren't just used to work out what is happening, they're also needed to send and receive messages – to communicate. Animals mostly use just three senses for communicating: sight, hearing and smell.

a howler monkey calling to its family group

harvest mice smelling each other

a peacock showing off its colourful feathers to find a partner

2 Sound messages

Sound is great for sending messages – sounds can be very loud, travel fast and cover long distances. The calls of some whales can travel an astonishing 6000 kilometres underwater – further than from London to New York!

All sounds are made by something vibrating – moving back and forward quickly. A good example is a guitar string, which vibrates when it is strummed. Sound vibrations travel through the air to the ears, vibrating the eardrum. The inside of the ear then detects this vibration, and sends a signal to the brain.

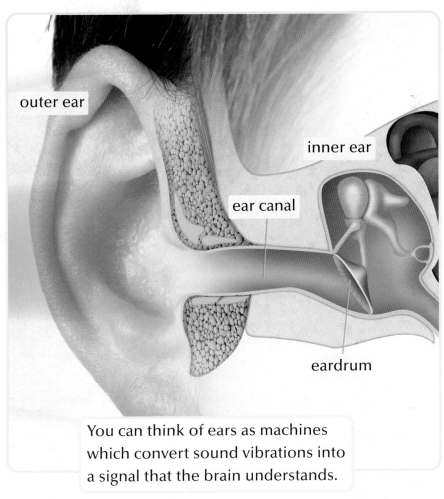

outer ear

inner ear

ear canal

eardrum

You can think of ears as machines which convert sound vibrations into a signal that the brain understands.

Finding your voice

Most **mammals**, including gorillas, chimpanzees and humans, can make sounds in the same way – using their voice box. This is two flaps of skin at the top of the windpipe. When breathing out, these flaps vibrate, creating sound. The mouth, tongue and lips then help to change the sound of a voice.

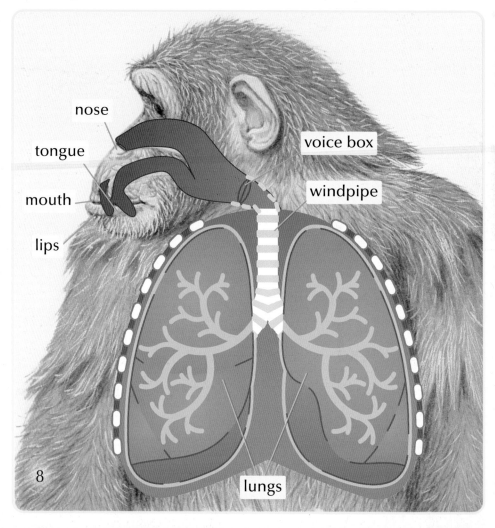

nose

tongue

mouth

lips

voice box

windpipe

lungs

Try it

Start humming and then open your mouth and move your tongue and lips – you should hear the sound of your voice change. If you put your hand on your throat you should be able to feel the vibrations of your voice box.

Lots of animals communicate with their voice: canaries sing, gibbons hoot, green frogs ribbet.

Grunting gorillas

They may not speak a full language like humans, but gorillas make about 22 different sounds or calls, and each has its own meaning!

Can you try speaking Gorilla?

belch: A low sound, like clearing your throat or coughing. This is the most common call gorillas make and shows they are relaxed and happy.

hoot: A high-pitched hoot that sounds like a monkey. This is a loud call, and gorillas use it to find their family in the forest.

young gorillas chuckling

grunt: A low snorting grunt. It's used to warn other gorillas away from a patch of food they are eating.

chuckle: This sounds just like human laughter. Gorillas chuckle to show they are enjoying playing with each other.

roar: A loud, aggressive roar. It's used to scare off other male gorillas from attacking their family group.

a male gorilla roaring

Beautiful birdsong

You can hear birdsong almost anywhere in the world, even in a busy city. Birds can make such beautiful sounds because they have two voice boxes. This means they can quickly switch between different notes, and even sing two notes at the same time. It is mostly male birds who sing – they do this to mark out their **territory**, but also to show off and impress female birds.

Nightingales look quite plain, but they're said to have the most beautiful song of any bird – famous poets have even written about it!

Birds have to learn how to sing their songs, just like human babies have to learn how to speak. Baby birds slowly practise and get better as they grow up, copying the sound of their parents.

A barking bird?

Lyrebirds, found in Australia, can copy sounds they hear in the wild. Lyrebirds have been heard making the calls of other types of birds, but also the sound of babies crying, phone calls and even dogs barking!

Noisy insects

Many insects also use sound to communicate, but they make their sounds in very different ways to gorillas and birds.

You might have heard the sound of crickets chirping in a grassy field. Crickets don't have voices, but use their wings to make sounds! Their wings have tiny scrapers on them which vibrate when rubbed together, creating sound. Male crickets make sounds for the same reason as birds – to mark out their territory, and impress females.

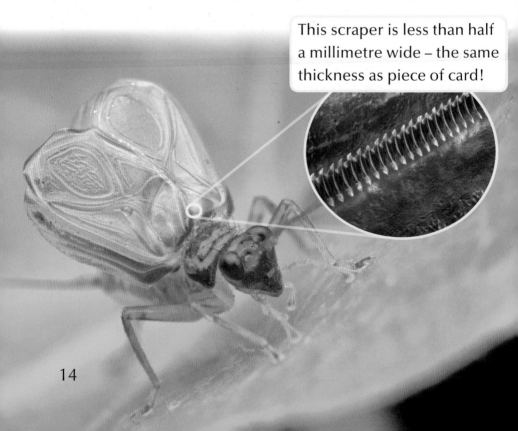

This scraper is less than half a millimetre wide – the same thickness as piece of card!

Madagascar hissing cockroaches are another noisy insect, but they make sound in a completely different way to crickets.

All insects use special holes along the side of their body to breathe in air. Hissing cockroaches can blast air through these holes, which creates a hissing sound. They hiss to warn others in their **colony** of danger, and also to scare away rivals.

a Madagascar hissing cockroach

3 Seeing messages

Light travels even faster than sound does – at almost 300,000 kilometres per second. At this speed, you could travel around the earth seven times in one second! As light shines down from the sun, it bounces or **reflects** off objects. Eyes then detect this light, which is how humans and animals see things.

Many animals use their body to communicate – moving their hands, doing a flashy dance or by a facial expression. This uses sight, because it is eyes that detect these movements.

The bright, colourful tail of a peacock is an unmissable visual signal.

Not all eyes are the same!

Some animals, like flatworms, can only see dark and light but no objects. Some, like nautiluses, have blurry vision and can just about see animals moving past them. Others, like octopuses, can see everything in clear detail just like we can.

octopus

nautilus

flatworm

Waving hello

In the noisy jungle, it can be difficult to hear sounds, so chimpanzees use movements to communicate – for others to see and understand.

Give me that. If a chimp wants something another chimp has, they will reach out with a flat hand.

***Groom** me.* If a chimp wants to be groomed, they will present that part of their body to another chimp.

Go away! If a chimp wants another chimp to go away, they will push them with a hand.

Hop on! If a parent wants their baby chimp to hop on their back for a ride, they will lift up their back foot.

Another animal that relies on movement to communicate are golden frogs. They live in the jungle next to loud waterfalls and so making sounds to scare away rivals wouldn't be heard. Instead, they sit up and wave an arm, making themselves look bigger to get rid of any intruders.

a golden frog

Beyond the rainbow

Human eyes can only detect some of the light which comes from the sun – the colours which make up the rainbow. But other animals can see more than this. Birds' eyes can also see ultraviolet light, which is just past violet on the rainbow.

This starling might not look very impressive to humans, but its feathers have an amazing pattern of bright colours when seen through a bird's eyes.

a European starling

Butterflies can also see ultraviolet light, and have colours on their wings, hidden to human eyes. Cabbage white butterflies look plain white to humans, but are a bright vibrant pink colour to other butterflies. Birds and butterflies use vibrant ultraviolet patterns to show off and impress others.

a cabbage white butterfly

Messages in the dark

Although there is no sunlight at night, some animals can still communicate using sight – by creating their own light!

Fireflies have special **molecules** inside their bodies which, when mixed, create a bright glow like a glowstick. There are lots of different **species** of fireflies, and each one flashes in a different pattern or colour. This flashing helps fireflies find each other in the dark night.

A firefly's yellow belly is where the glow is produced.

The ocean is filled with animals which create their own light. On some beaches, the waves seem to glow bright blue. But this is actually plankton – tiny creatures less than one millimetre long. These plankton flash when they're attacked; other nearby plankton see this flashing and copy it. Together, their bright flashing scares away predators.

Together, many small plankton can make waves glow blue.

Firefly squids put on an even more impressive light show, with blue and green flashing spots all over their bodies. Once a year, thousands of them gather together to find a partner. This flashing not only helps them to find each other in the dark, but also to impress their potential partners.

firefly squid

4 Smelly signals

Our world is filled with smells: freshly-cut grass, baking cakes, a smoky fire. Amazingly, we smell things because tiny molecules of the thing land on the inside of our noses. The nose then sends signals to the brain which works out what the smell is.

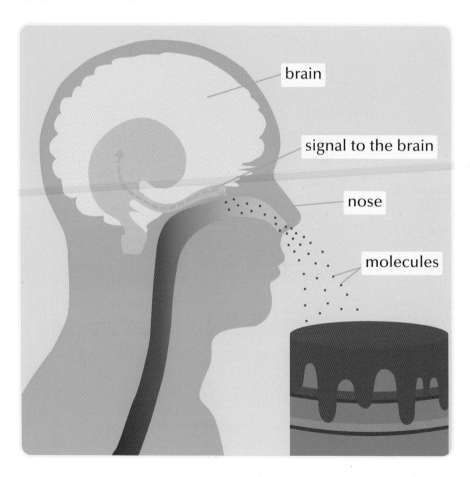

brain

signal to the brain

nose

molecules

Smell is much slower than sight or hearing because molecules have to drift through the air and reach noses. This means that it is not possible to send complicated, detailed messages with smells.

Yet lots of animals do use smell to communicate, such as dogs. They urinate on places they think of as their territory, such as gardens. When other dogs smell this stinky urine, it gives them a simple message: *keep out!*

Like this dog, many animals warn off competition with their urine.

Sounding the alarm

Many insects communicate using smells, including aphids. These are tiny leaf-eating insects which are found on plants – hundreds all at once. Aphids are often attacked by wasps, but when this happens, the aphids release a special molecule that others can smell. This is like an alarm – as soon as other aphids smell this molecule, they run away from it, hopefully escaping attack.

a colony of aphids on a plant

Sending an alarm signal is the most common way smell is used to communicate. Unfortunately for aphids, wasps have learnt to smell their alarm molecule. If they smell it, they know that there must be aphids nearby to attack. Life as an insect is never easy!

This wasp is about to attack an aphid.

Follow the leader

Ants communicate with smelly molecules too, but in a very different way. Most ants live in underground **colonies** containing thousands of ants, and they work together to gather food to feed everyone. Every day, worker ants leave the colony looking for food. When an ant finds food, it leaves a trail of smelly molecules as it walks back to the nest. This makes it easy for the other ants to find the same patch of food.

As more ants travel along this trail, they add more molecules to it, making the smell stronger and the path easier to follow. This is why you often see ants walking in a long line – they are all following the same smelly trail.

Super-smellers

Snakes have one of the best senses of smell of all animals,
and it's the reason for their flicking tongues. Snakes don't
just use their nose for smelling – they have another **organ**
in the roof of their mouth, called the Jacobson's organ,
which helps them smell too. Snakes flick their tongues
in and out to bring smells into their mouth, towards their
Jacobson's organ.

flicking their tongue
helps snakes to smell

A snake's tongue is Y-shaped, which means it can tell if it is smelling something on its left or right side. This helps snakes to work out where a smell is coming from, giving them a very accurate sense of smell. Snakes smell each other to check who is in their family. Smelly trails left by adult snakes help their young to follow them to good spaces for **hibernating**.

Snakes sometimes gather in large groups, so smell is important when you need to find the right snake!

5 What about us?

It's clear animals communicate in some impressive ways –
from the smells of tiny ants to the sounds of giant whales.
But what about us humans? How do our senses compare to
those in the animal kingdom?

Smell

We humans don't really use our sense of smell for
communication, and so it isn't that good. Dogs use their sense
of smell a lot, and so it is 10,000 times better than ours!

Nosing around

You can usually spot animals with a good sense of smell by
their big noses. Almost half of a dog's head is its nose!

Sight

Humans have quite good eyesight and can see details that many other animals can't. **Birds of prey** have even better eyesight than us – meaning they can spot food on the ground when flying high in the sky.

a wedge-tailed eagle spotting prey while flying

Hearing

The hearing of humans is also very good – better than a lot of animals. But some animals, such as elephants, can hear much lower sounds than we can. The deep, low sounds elephants make can travel many kilometres, helping them communicate across the desert.

an African elephant

35

Language

Humans have one thing which no animal can beat: language. Language helps people work together, to build communities and to share knowledge and ideas. It's one reason why humans have spread all across the world. There might be different languages used around the world, but we can learn these and communicate with everyone.

We can even use sign language to communicate with people who have problems with their hearing.

6 Talking with animals

Animals don't just communicate with each other.
They communicate with us too! Dogs can understand and
follow simple instructions from humans. When you tell
a dog to sit, it doesn't just hear the word you have said,
it also sees you are pointing to the floor, and hears from
the **tone** of your voice that you have made a command.
It uses all this information together to understand you.

Some parrots not only learn what some words mean, but
they also speak those words at the right time. These parrots
have learnt to say hello, ask for their favourite foods, and
even ask their owners to be quiet!

Humans communicate with cats
without even realising it.
Cats can use their hearing
and vision to work out
how you are feeling.
It's the reason
they come to sit
on your lap when
you're feeling sad!

Chimpanzees are perhaps the animal that humans can communicate with the most. Since chimpanzees use lots of different movements to communicate in the wild, scientists have managed to teach some chimpanzees to use human sign language. This means they can have a real conversation – asking the chimps what they want to do, what they want to eat or how they are feeling. This is an amazing achievement, but some scientists think that we shouldn't be training chimpanzees like this, and that they should spend their time with other chimpanzees and not humans.

a family of chimpanzees in the wild

A wonderful world of communication

From the flutter of a bird's wings to the laughter of a gorilla, communication is vital for animals' survival. They use it to form friendships, create family groups and work together, just like humans do.

The next time you are outside, why not take a moment to see what you can discover. If you're in the woods, see if you can spot any colourful birds.

If you are in a field, perhaps you can hear some insects? Maybe even stop and give a tree a good sniff if you're feeling brave! You might be amazed at all the animal messages you find!

Glossary

birds of prey Birds with sharp beaks and claws which hunt other animals

colony/colonies a group or groups of animals which live together and help each other out

groom when animals spend time removing insects and dirt from each other's bodies

hibernating animals sleeping through the winter to save energy

mammals warm-blooded animals that have a backbone and grow hair, and feed their young with milk from the mother

molecules tiny pieces of something. Molecules join together to make up everything.

organ a part of the body that does a particular job

predator an animal that eats other animals

reflects the act of light or sound bouncing off something

species a group of the same living things that can breed with each other.

territory the area of land where an animal lives

tone the features of a sound – high or low, loud or soft, smooth or rough

Index

Hearing

Gorillas chuckle and grunt.

Birds sing.

Cockroaches hiss.

Humans talk.

Sight

Chimpanzees make movements.

Fireflies flash.

Golden frogs wave.

Smell

Aphids release molecules.

Ants leave a trail.

Snakes flick their tongues.

 Ideas for reading

Written by Gill Matthews
Primary Literacy Consultant

Reading objectives:
- check that the text makes sense to them, discuss their understanding and explain the meaning of words in context
- ask questions to improve their understanding of a text
- identify main ideas drawn from more than one paragraph and summarise these
- retrieve and record information from non-fiction

Spoken language objectives:
- articulate and justify answers, arguments and opinions
- use spoken language to develop understanding through speculating, hypothesising, imagining and exploring ideas

Curriculum links: Science – Living things and their habitats

Interest words: language, communities, knowledge

Resources: IT

Build a context for reading

- Ask children to look at the front cover. Discuss the title. What do children think the answer might be?
- Ask children what kind of book they think this is. Encourage them to support their responses with reasons and evidence.
- Read the back-cover blurb. Confirm that this is an information book. Discuss what features the book might have.
- Give children time to skim through the book to spot the features that are typical of information texts.

Understand and apply reading strategies

- Ask children to find the contents page. Read the title of the first chapter and ask children what they think *communication* is.
- Read pp2–5 aloud. Ask children what they think communication is, having read this chapter. Demonstrate how to summarise the information in the chapter.

- Allocate Chapters 2, 3 and 4 to children to read. Once they have read their chapter they can make notes that summarise the information. Take feedback from this activity.
- Give children time to read Chapters 5 and 6. Ask them what the three most interesting facts are that they have learnt.

Develop reading and language comprehension

- Discuss children's responses to the book. Explore what they particularly enjoyed about it and whether they have any questions about it.
- Ask children to read pp46–47 and to choose one of the senses listed. They can then go back into the book, find the information that is given on pp46–47 and find out why animals do these things.
- Read pp36–37. Explore children's understanding of the interest words. Explore the questions on page 36.

Support a creative response

- Children can find out more about sign language and learn some greeting signs.
- Children can choose one of the animals mentioned in the book and find out more about its habitat and diet. Their research can be presented as fact files.
- Children can keep a communication diary for a day where they list the different ways they communicate with other people.

Read more

Code Making, Code Breaking (Emerald/Band 15) is another information book about the world of communication and codes.

Emeral•
Band 15

Collins
BIG CAT

Can I talk to a chimpanzee?

Come on a scientific safari and explore the amazing ways
animals communicate with each other, from grunting gorillas
and whale calls to copycat birds and smelly snakes.

ISBN 978-0-00-847894-0

9 780008 478940 >

collins.co.uk/collinsbigcat

Ri **The Royal Institution**
Science Lives Here

An information book

CHRISTOPHER BROWN
Accidental Detective

Valerie Bloom

Monique Steele

Collins
BIG CAT

Published by Collins
An imprint of HarperCollins*Publishers*

The News Building
1 London Bridge Street
London SE1 9GF
UK

Macken House,
39/40 Mayor Street Upper,
Dublin 1, DO1 C9W8,
Ireland

10 9 8 7 6 5 4 3

ISBN 978-0-00-847882-7

British Library Cataloguing-in-Publication Data
A catalogue record for this publication is available from the British Library.

Author: Valerie Bloom
Illustrator: Monique Steele (Illo Agency)
Reading ideas author: Gill Matthews
Publisher: Lizzie Catford
Commissioning editor: Leilani Sparrow
Product manager: Sarah Thomas
Project manager: Emily Hooton
Copyeditor: Sally Byford
Proofreader: Gaynor Spry
Typesetter: 2Hoots Publishing Services Ltd
Cover designer: 2Hoots Publishing Services Ltd
Production controller: Katharine Willard

Collins would like to thank The Python Hill Academy for their part in the development of this book.

Printed and bound in the UK using 100% Renewable Electricity at Martins the Printers Ltd.

MIX
Paper | Supporting
responsible forestry
FSC
www.fsc.org   FSC™ C007454

Get the latest Collins Big Cat news at
collins.co.uk/collinsbigcat